The Bears & Other Poems

Knute Skinner

Acknowledgements

Some of the poems in this collection have appeared in the following publications: *Ambit, Amelia, Cyphers, Hatbox, Hobo Jungle, The Hollins Critic, Imago, Inside Outside, The Malahat Review, Nahant Bay, The New York Quarterly, Permafrost, Poetry Australia, Poetry Ireland Review, The Quarterly, Roughly Speaking, The Salmon, Southern Review, Trees of the Fians: Departures 3, The University of Windsor Review, Visions International, Weyfarers, Writing in the West and Zone 3.*

Cover Etching by Vincent Sheridan, Courtesy of
Gilvarry Geoghegan Gallery
Cover Design by Johan Hofsteenge
Typeset by Nova Print, Galway
Printed by Colour Books Ltd., Dublin
Hardback Binding by Kenny's Fine Binding, Galway

ISBN 0 948339 72 1 Hardcover £8.50 - $12.95
ISBN 0 948339 73 X Softcover £4.95 - $7.95

Salmon Publishing, The Bridge Mills, Galway

The characters in these poems are all fictitious.

*To the members of
the North Clare Writers Workshop*

Contents

The Bears

Not my father but my mother.
That's who you see on the footpath,
holding my hand while I look at the bears.

Old and overexposed.
The snapshot, I mean, not my mother.
About her, I can nothing say.
I was still in pipe curls.

I do remember the bears.
They were large and dark and I didn't like
their heavy, deliberate movements.
When one of them came near the barrier,
Mother tightened her grip and said,
'Do you see the bear?'

Mother looks like a bear herself in that long dark coat.
Of course it would make you think
that she was my father.

But it wasn't even my father who took the picture.
He was gone by then - somewhere in South America.
If he had taken the picture, it would be in focus.

Before

'I have been here before,' she said.
I looked out on the path,
a just discernible mark
in the rocks and tall grasses.
It sloped down, I knew,
toward hidden stretches of sand.
'I have too,' I said, after a brief pause,
'but then that's obvious, isn't it?
I mean, since I drove us here.'
She touched her fingertips to my cheek.
'Hush,' she said, smiling. 'It doesn't matter.'

Later, stretched out on the blanket,
our bodies, recently joined, lay separate except
where our hands retained the connection.
It was a rare late summer afternoon
with the sky so clear you could almost see through it
and the sea so quiet it was scarcely there.
What I wanted to say was I love you.

'Who was with you?' I said.
She turned toward me, puzzled,
and the sun glistened in the drops of moisture
on her neck and breasts.
'I mean,' I said, 'on those times
you were here before.'

'Oh, no one you know,' she said.
She smiled again, and her eyes
were as clear as the sky.
I have been here before, I said to myself.
'It doesn't matter,' she said, and she laughed
as she dribbled a handful of sand
over my stomach.

Blowups

It was still there two hours later,
just where Rita had found it,
and where she had left it.

It was scarcely approachable,
so fraught was the close air with the stench of death,
but she did take me to within a few feet.

Rita said she would call the officers later,
but it was a matter of some importance first
for me to click a few pictures.

As we picked our way back through the scrubs and brambles,
we heard a distant screech, like that
of some small animal under attack.

Rita has her own idea of a good joke.
At the big do she had last night for my birthday,
there were large blowups all over her patio walls.

The Bottom of the Fifth

My eyes followed his to the window.
A year's accumulation of smoke and grease
filtered the already muted
colours of the alley.
We had said one year.

I stood there a long minute
while the line of his profile hardened.
I could hear from the radio in his office
that the Cubs had a runner on second
in the bottom of the fifth.

Though the money was mine to take,
I was hesitating.
It no longer seemed like enough.

But it does go a long way here in Santa Cruz.
It buys a lot of drinks for my young friends
as I sit out a sequel of golden days
under these slow and capacious
blue skies.

The Bright Shiners

My host was silent for a moment or two,
but that no longer surprised me.
His store of small talk, it had turned out,
was painfully small.
Was this the same man whose blue eyes
shone bright as he quoted Maslow?
Who ran his hand through his mop of blond hair
as he leaned toward us over the lectern
and covered us all in a shower of words?

Allowing that he may not have heard me the first time,
I asked him again if he found us an interesting class.
This time he smiled and he cleared his throat
and he pulled at his tie and he took a drink of water.
Then he said that he hadn't decided,
that it was too soon to tell.

In the silence that followed I turned my attention
to the gleam of the tableware,
which reflected light from a candle in a glass dish.
I picked up a spoon, one of the bright shiners,
and saw myself on its bowl, distorted of course.
What he saw, if he noticed, was a nervous young woman,
overly dressed as if for church
and not for dinner at a seaside cafe.

We got through the meal somehow,
talking mostly about the good food,
but I'd have given him my soul
for a glass of wine.
As far as my body was concerned,
he did come close once -
ushering me toward his car -
to touching my elbow.

Later that night I gave my roommates
a few good laughs at his expense,
for which even now I feel guilty.
I'd assumed that what he had in mind
was getting me into his bed,
but who knows, maybe there was something else.
The only time he spoke while driving me home
was to tell me a joke about the dean.
I didn't get it at first, and he had to explain it.

The Car

The car moved off with its burden,
leaving Gary and me behind
on the town's main drag.
We made note of the telephone booth
by the Texaco station,
then crossed to the Any Time Bar and Grill
where we ordered beers.

The place was empty except for the waitress
and a burly old fart who sat reading
The Rocky Mountain News.
The waitress called him Walter
when she refilled his coffee,
and he grunted a vague thanks
behind his paper.

The name on her tag was Helen.
She was an ash blonde
with dark hair roots and a stricken face,
but under all that a more than adequate body.
Gary began straightening his tie
and running a hand through his hair
just out of habit.
She wasn't showing a bit of interest,
and we had our schedule.

I finished my Coors and moved to the cash register
where a sign on the wall announced
that because of AIDS
the staff were no longer required to kiss
the boss's ass.
I picked out a candy bar in a yellow wrapper
and paid for our beer.

The sun had by now gone past its peak
and begun its long hot drop
to the distant foothills.
The car was by now parked out in the desert.
We crossed through the dust sweeping along the road,
and we made our phone call.

Claude

Claude walked over to the fire and stood warming his hands,
a measure of satisfaction inserted
into his bland and hardy expression.
The wood he had chopped was stacked neatly
outside my door,
and I had to be grateful that he had saved me
some hours of tedious labour.

There'd be a tariff of course,
beginning at once with a show of thanks
and proceeding in stages.
I managed what I supposed was a smile
and puckered my mouth to blow him a kiss.
He seemed to find this enough for the moment.
The days were short this time of year,
and the night would inevitably be a long one.

We sat down then to the bare wood table,
and I dished up deliberately small portions
of the stew I put together
from the brace of rabbits he brought me.
To make the meal last even longer
I uncorked a second bottle
of my blackcurrant wine.
As usual, we had little to talk about.

But in time we finished the meal,
and once he had dried the last dish I produced
from the bucket of sudsy water,
he stretched me over the same wood table
and began in his abrupt, rough way.
Once again the winds in my sails were unfavourable,

and the mates gave each other surreptitious glances
as if to affirm that the crew fomented
a drastic, precipitant act.
This rough passage is from my perspective of course.
From his, he was firm in command of the surge,
through it all a good sailor.

Claude's cabin, though I have never been there,
is five miles around the bend in the river.
Mine is the only other cabin about,
and we can't even see the smoke from each other's fires.
Claude has to be alone as much as I am,
but always he waits for me
to invite him over.

Clumsy

The boy shut the door behind him
and twisted around.
Clumsy as he was, his young body
was a pure show
of honeysweet motion -
fetching and tempting
as a plate of well cooked rabbit.
Oh Cupid had brought me a cupful
of love in that one.
I could see he was already ready.

It was a late summer evening
with millers beating hard on the windows
and the fan moving hot air around
inside the trailer.
My forehead was wet with sweat
and my dress sticking damp to my shoulders.
I opened two bottles of Bud,
but they were gone warm
by the time we drank them.

The cat had ahold of his tongue, I guess.
He didn't say two words - he got right to work -
but he cussed a bit when his fingers
stumbled over my buttons.
I'd have done them quicker, but he once said
he liked opening me up.
I was like a gift, he once said,
inside a package.
A big enough gift, I suppose,
but he told me he sure liked it.

We did it the one time only,
him on top for a change.
He grunted a lot, and when he came
he sort of laughed, but it was mostly
like he was choking.
When he finished, he buried his face
in my Big Berthas.
He hadn't bothered to shave, but somehow
I didn't say one word about it.
There was something that strange
in and around him.

Well, we drank our beers and all at once
he started to cry like a baby.
I laid my hand on his leg, but he pulled away
and got back quick inside of
his jeans and shoes.
He was carrying his shirt, going out the door.
I didn't get dressed, and after a time
I turned on the gas and warmed up some coffee.

Well, that was the time he got fired from his job
for ruining most of a stack of boards.
In the morning he was gone off.

Company for Christmas

We had plenty of company for Christmas that year.
Dan and his wife Blanche drove up from Kentucky,
bringing a ham and several bottles of whiskey
as well as their three little girls.
Kay, their eldest, was in her first year of school then,
and Mollie was four, and Millie was two and a half.

And Bob's brother Burt arrived with Sarah,
the woman he took up with when Ruthie divorced him.
They came by train all the way from their ranch in Wyoming,
with a toddler, Mike, and their newborn baby, Jennie.
That Jennie was a good baby and she never cried.

With our own three kids we had quite a houseful, I tell you.
Mother was still alive then,
and Uncle William was living just down the road.
And of course Bob's parents were with us.

It was a happy time then, I tell you.
We had plenty of good things to eat,
and we laughed a lot, remembering, and we played games,
and we even sang carols on Christmas Eve.
The little ones built such a funny-looking snowman
that Rascal spent a day barking under the porch.
Dan, to give him credit, never drank too much,
and he and Blanche got along just fine.
Mother cried a lot but only because she was happy.

There's more to tell, if I tell it all.
Dan and Burt helped Bob repair
the broken bannister on the basement steps,
and Sarah was a big help to me in the kitchen.

She's a sweet girl and Burt can call himself lucky.
Uncle William made a fine speech on Christmas,
remembering Daddy, who had died that summer.

But I mustn't forget the presents.
There were never so many under one tree.
Most of them were toys and clothes for the children,
but the rest of us all got something from everybody else.
Bob's present to me was the loveliest watch
that I ever did see or ever hope to see.
I wanted to keep it safe in its box,
but Bob said he wanted me to wear it,
and it's still running to this day.

I guess it's running better than the rest of us,
I mean those of us who are only just ticking.
Dan and Blanche seem to be doing the best,
though we don't get word very often.
Burt's doctor says his cancer is in remission,
so I guess it means there's still hope,
and we're all thankful for that.
Bob and I are doing all right, though he's got kind of funny
since he had the accident cleaning out the garage.
It was nothing serious, but it does seem
to have made him awful quiet.
Some days my arthritis is bad, but I don't complain.

I suppose the whole lot of us -
Dan, Blanche, Burt, Sarah, and Bob and me -
spend a lot of useless time fretting
about what our kids have got up to.
But that, as they say, is another story.

I find myself a lot of the time any more
thinking about that last Christmas with Mother
and all of the company we had.

Crocodiles

Louise shook her head sadly
and pushed her cup in my direction.
I reached for the pot of herb tea,
which was nearly empty.

'This may be strong,' I said, pouring.

'It makes no difference,' she said.
'It's all the same.'

She hadn't been crying,
but even so she was pale and drained,
a spectre amid the colours of my patio.

'He wasn't as advertised,' she said
and drank from her cup.
She had said this already, twice.
'When it came time for Sam to deliver the goods,
he wasn't as advertised
and I wanted him out, out, out.'

I closed my eyes and summoned my help.
In a moment a myriad of crocodiles,
erect on their tails, pranced up and down a meadow.
Their eyes were laughing
and they called me to join in.

When I opened my eyes, I again saw Louise.
She was staring across the garden at Clifford,
who had come out from the greenhouse
and was walking toward us.

It isn't fair of me, I suppose,
to be so happy.

Dawn

At the first sign of dawn bust,
I stood by the newly planted sorghum
and helped Mae to her feet.
The moon was mooching its way toward Thorsten's stables.
She laughed and straightened my collar.
I picked a straw from the shoulder of her T-shirt,
letting my fingers linger.

At the fork in the service road
where our ways parted,
she kicked at a stone in the grass,
setting a dozen grasshoppers in motion.
'We've done it now,' she said, biting her thumb.
I saw a light come on in an upstairs window.
'Yes,' I agreed, 'we've done it.'

A Day Out

She turned her back to me -
graceful, ivory.
'Darling, can you zip me up?'

I set down the racing form,
grumbling a bit but pleased
with the assignment.
She only laughed when I tried to kiss her
and smear her lipstick.

She laughed again at the track,
even when we lost big
on the beaten favourite.
I was proud of how good she looked
in the dress she made.

At Sarducci's we ate salmon
and fettucini.
We ordered a second carafe
of white Chianti,
and we held hands on the table.
When my eyes moved to her neck,
I thought of the zipper.
'Have I told you today,' she said,
'how much I love you?'

I'm in bed now - engulfed and drained -
with the taste of her body in my mouth.
She's running her fingers over
what's left of my hair
and whispering the words of a song.
In a minute or two I'll get up

and make tea,
and I'll offer a toast to us
and the next ten years.

A Death in Summer

I can't explain this part very well.
We were supposed to be looking
for sheep on the mountain.

There were stones piled in heaps,
vague disturbed shapes in the dark.
Shapes, but not sheep, on the mountain.

There were sounds of the night,
not birdcall or creaking branch or rustle of leaves -
not the sound of sheep -
but muffled speech and bodies
in close collision.

The hand gripping mine held tight.
The legs of my small brother faltered.
'Toni, I'm scared.'

The hand gripping *mind* held tight.
But I wasn't ready to be stayed.
I went on alone.

What I found then and there
and what I came back to
I still breathe hard to relate.

I can't explain this part very well.
It wasn't sheep on the mountain.

The Door

I had been pounding on the door
for over a minute,
but I wasn't going to give up.
I like pounding on doors.

And I knew Candy was in there.
She was sitting on the bed,
painting her goddammed toenails,
in one of her moods.

Or she was twisting around on that bed,
wrapped in a pair of sweaty arms.
The horny kid who worked at the bakery,
the laid-off welder in 17B.

Or she was sleeping it off,
the empty bottle dead in the dust balls,
the glass at the tips of her fingers.

Or she was dead herself,
a rose-red pill box exhausted
on the bedside table.

Well, it made me no never mind.
I'd knock till my goddammed knuckles were bloody.
I'd knock till I raised the dead.

The Evening Something or Other

He shampoos his receding hair in a listless fashion
while I read to him from the *Herald-Trib*.
The wars of the world hold no interest for Joseph,
only its values.

From my perch on the plastic toilet seat,
I can look up at his puffy, pallid bottom.
It's set off now by a painful red
on his legs and back.
He's had it with the beach, he tells me.

He steps out of the shower and takes the paper,
refusing the towel I offer.
When he sits on the edge of the bed,
I watch water drip from his bulging gut
onto the carpet.
In this heat he'll be dry in a minute, he tells me,
and I run the water for my bath.

Outside, the bells of a dozen churches
announce the evening something or other.
I no longer try to imagine what they're saying.
The bells speak Spanish.

And he's too sore to sit through the concert, he says.
After dinner we'll go to another bodega,
and then I suppose that once again
we'll close down the hotel lounge.

He's on the telephone now to New York,
and I'm lying back in the tub, gazing at tiles.
I soap my breasts as I hear him selling
some shares in something or other.

Flowers for Aunt Alma

'I told you,' he said, 'when we picked up your flowers,
it was still raining like a cow taking a piss
on a flat rock.'
Baxter pushed in the lighter and stepped on the gas.
'And that's why we didn't get out to the graveyard.'
He threw the wrapper from his cigar
out the car window.
'And if that's going to bother Aunt Alma,
then it's too damned bad.'

I said nothing more - what was the point? -
but shrank into the back seat, dreading
the smell of his smoke.

'And as Lucy here is my witness, just ask Lucy,' -
he jerked his cigar in Lucy's direction -
'it was too wet to go traipsing out to her grave.
Aunt Alma wouldn't expect it, not even from you.'
He dragged out the *ou* in *you*.
'No siree,' he said, 'not in that weather.'

If Lucy nodded her head, I didn't notice.
I was looking instead at the arrangement
which shared the back seat.
It had cost me my half day's pay,
but Aunt Alma always did love flowers.

'You can give that bouquet to Mother,' Baxter said,
pointing the burning cigar back over his shoulder.
His voice softened to a silky insinuation.
'It's better to do for the living,' he said,
'and the living can do for you.'

My eyes were smarting now, and I dug
in my bag for a tissue.

'And don't tell me again that Aunt Alma's
turning over in her grave.
You've turned that poor woman in her grave so many times
she's forgotten which way they put her in.
Isn't that right, Lucy?' Then he let out his laugh,
which was more an explosive snort than a laugh.
'Well, isn't it, Lucy?' he asked again.

'Yes,' replied Lucy in almost a whisper,
without moving her head.
'Yes, I suppose so.'

'You're goddamned right about that,' said Baxter
as he slowed down to turn into Mother's driveway.
'Auntie can hardly turn over in her grave again.
She's got herself all tangled up by now
in the satin lining.'

Friday Evening

The fog swirled over the heads
of the marching men.
They were approaching
Antietam.
I switched the channel.

A woman was showing her dumb husband
a new product.
It costs a lot less
or maybe it's pennies more but worth it.
Anyway their dog ate it.

I stretched and walked into the kitchen.
Philip would be on his way over.
I basted the chicken and added the new potatoes.
I could toss the salad later
and put on the beans.

The dog was gone now, and in its place
old Ronnie addressed the nation.
He wanted more of my money for the Contras.
I sat down on the bed
and brushed out my hair.

Last Friday Phillip brought me a bottle
of Blue Nun.
After dinner we played Scrabble
before we made love,
and then we caught the last of the *The Best of Carson.*

Harmony

'I'd like to be alone with her,' Vicki said
at the entrance to Harmony's room.
'So would I,' I answered, pushing past Vicki
and shutting the door on her perfect
but surprised face.

I don't know if Vicki listened at the door or not,
but probably she ran right off
to broadcast at large her incondensable grief.
There was never a mix of heart in the rubblework
that made up my little Vicki.

If she did listen, she wouldn't have heard a lot,
at least not at first.
Harmony was wailing out loud
like an infant reacting to baptism,
and it took me some tiresome minutes to shut her down.
This gave me time to scrutinize her room.

It was much as I had imagined -
all puffy and pink -
and now that I think of it, so was Harmony herself.

I had my way with her then, as people say,
but it wasn't a way to inspire
commemoration.
Harmony as a lover had yet to earn
her union card,
and the transports she effected in me then
were barely worth the freightage
of Vicki's displeasure.

You have the rest of it, I believe,
now that Vicki's turned writer,
but she couldn't have told you that Harmony's aptitude
has passed all tests;
and it's not in Vicki's interest, I feel sure,
to let you know how well the three of us
get on together.

Hilary

Then I took off the rest of my clothing, and I went back in
to the sitting room.
Where Hilary should have been waiting, eager,
on the divan.
Or waiting somewhere at least. Eager.

Well now, I thought, where could Hilary have gone?
After me going to so much trouble
to get myself ready?
Hilary's gone to the loo, I suppose.
(That's how I answered myself.)

Hilary's shoes were lying in the middle
of the braided rug,
in front of the fire (which was coming on strong now).
Hilary's glass, now empty, lay on its side
on the hardwood floor.
I picked up the shoes and placed them both neatly
in front of the glassed-in bookcase.
(Just at the middle of the works of Charles Dickens.)
I picked up the glass and placed it on the mantelpiece,
on top of a coaster,
next to my own empty glass (on another coaster).

Then, turning around, I spotted Hilary's socks.
They were draped over the large oil painting
of the Swedish deer park
which my parents brought back from some
extravagant impulse.
One sock hung over the side displaying the river.
And one hung over the side displaying the woods.
The deer were grazing in between.

Well, when I pulled them off, I noticed some dust
gathering along the top of the painting's frame,
and I wiped it carefully off with one of the socks
(a sock with a small hole in the toe).
Then, with a sock in each hand, I started to dust
around the two glasses on the mantelpiece
and to wipe down the tiles at the sides of the fireplace.
Then, carefully lifting the shades just an inch or two,
I used Hilary's socks to wipe off the window sills.
(Serves Hilary right, I thought, for not being here.)
Then I tucked those socks neatly in Hilary's shoes
and stood looking around.

The braided rug had a wrinkle, and I straightened it out
with my bare right foot.
The slip cover on the armchair looked soiled.
I made a note to take care of that in the morning.
The door to the closet was standing ajar,
just a few inches open,
and I crossed the room with a sigh.

Then, just as I grabbed the doorknob, what did I see
but a cuff of my fur coat down on the floor,
sticking out an inch and a half (or so) from the closet.
Well I threw open the door and what did I see?
All of the coats in a tumble on the closet floor.
Not only my coats but my scarves and a shawl
and some of the skirts that I keep in that closet.
They were all in a tumble, and I squatted down
to gather them up.

Then Hilary's laugh was right there in my ears,
and Hilary's right hand (probably) was closing tight
on my left arm,
pulling me into the closet
and down on the floor.
Before I could say any more than 'Oh Hilary',
Hilary had me sprawling there on my back.
On all those coats and skirts and scarves.
(And on the shawl too, of course.)
(And on Hilary's clothing too, as it turned out.)

'I thought,' said Hilary, on top of me now
and speaking in a funny sort of a voice
(like a voice made up for a part in a play),
'you were never, never, never, never, never
going to find me.'

The House Guest

She tapped a spoon to the rim
of her empty glass.
'Robby?' she said, speaking as if to the spoon.
'What is it?' I asked her.
'Oh, nothing.'

I looked at the brown fleck in her left blue eye
and then at the knee of my corduroy pants
where the pile had worn smooth.
One image told me about as much
as the other.

A moment passed and she resumed
tapping the glass.
I offered more wine but she shook her head.
I saw that blackbirds were lining themselves up
on the telephone wire.

Soon they were all in a line
that would have made a picture,
but I had no camera.
They scattered quickly as I stood up
to clear the table.

When I returned with coffee and Drambuie,
I found her leaning on the old oak
at the end of the garden.
Her right arm, in a line above her shoulder,
had pulled one side of her blouse loose from her jeans.

In front of her, the sky was putting on
one of its slow western sunsets.
It framed the tree and it framed her body.
'I was going to ask,' she said, turning around,
'if there's anything good at the movies.'

Hushed

Suddenly he hushed me
and we sat in his car not moving.
I never saw anyone listen so hard.

He was sometimes like that in the diner,
letting the coffee I served him
grow cold in his hand,

but there, there was always something
he could listen in on,
and he never finished his coffee anyhow.

One thing was for sure, whatever he thought he heard,
I couldn't hear it -
and my shoulders were getting cold.

I wanted to say, 'Let's get this show on the road,'
but whatever was happening in his head
was just too weird.

I wanted to tell my dead mother
that if she got me out of this one,
I'd be a good girl.

Incense

It started with incense,
or rather with the memory of incense,
there on the footpath where I
went walking with Beth.

'What are you thinking of now?' she asked,
playfully butting her forehead
against my shoulder.
'Nothing. Oh, nothing,' I lied
as I lifted her chin and kissed her.

It was just half a lie,
for the incense, just then, was only
half of a memory.

The banks were a riot of colour,
and the odour of bloom fell heavy
on the night air,
but the paths by the river were wet
from a late spring rain.
This night we would have to forego
lying at our ease.

Well, soon we would have
our own bed to lie on,
and papered walls complete
with designs of flowers,
and only a chance breeze
at the curtained window
to bear the weight of incense,
or rather its memory.

The Interview

The interview seemed over,
and I had the unfortunate feeling
that it had never begun.

Mr. Someone (Brophy?) sat there
lining up the edges of his notes,
stacking them neat on the table.
He hadn't even asked me
if I had any questions,
and never once did he look
in my grey-green eyes.

On the wall hung a framed picture
of Ralph Waldo Emerson,
sharing government space
with George and with Honest Abe.
Benign old father
afloat in your oversoul,
what were you doing there?

Could you see through the high window
the rosaceous trees in blossom?
or the small craft that passed
slow on the turgid river?

Mr. Someone, you had me stacked,
neat on your neat table.
You knew all you wanted to know.
But you never once saw my eyes.
You never heard my questions.
Do you mind if I straighten your tie?
Are those your own teeth?
What are you doing for lunch?

In the Bathroom

She lurched through the house to the bathroom,
and I followed after her as best I could,
depending as I do on my cane.
When I arrived I found her gasping,
bent over the toilet and holding the wall for support.
I put an arm gently around her waist,
and I placed a hand on her forehead, holding back her red hair.
'There, there, honey,' I said. 'There, there.'

That was two years ago today.
We were in one of the downstairs bathrooms,
the one we had painted green the month before.
The towels, nearly new, were a bright white
and edged in yellow.
A late evening sun came pouring in
through the curtains our daughter Judy made for our birthdays
(our birthdays are both in May).

I don't go into that bathroom any more,
though guests are free to use it.
I don't believe in giving
power to the past.
I mean by that, that I haven't
kept any of her clothing.
Whatever Judy didn't want went straight to Goodwill.
I haven't made a shrine of her dressing table
or done anything like that.

But I don't go into that bathroom.
For days after, I could still hear our spaniel pup
whimpering in the doorway,
and I couldn't erase the sight of those green walls
and the red blood in the toilet.

The Knocking

I was doing the Half Butterfly when the knocking
came at the door,
polite at first, then persistent,
the thrusting language of knuckles on wood.

Later, after meditation, I looked out the window
and became what I saw -
below, the white thorn petals
which scattered on the green yard,
above, one middy blouse of a cloud,
bright white on an eye-blue sky.

I have found no explanation for the urgent caller,
no note on the door, no token,
no follow-up phone call.
Whoever walked the path in from the gate
exists in his or her own time, not mine,
and no theory of what I missed
has eclipsed those affinities
which made my day.

The Latch-Key

The child followed Ann to the house.
Was it a boy or a girl? she wondered.
One might as well ask if dogs
have a sense of humour,
or what is the true redemptive value
of burning nettles.
Only the Angel of Death, Ann decided,
would have the answers.

The child, though obviously unwell,
stood gamely erect
as Ann fingered the zoo in her
leather handbag
to locate her urgent latch-key.
Well, whom could she ask, she decided,
if it had a home?
Wasn't she a stranger in Tejas?

Weeks later and a hemisphere apart,
she told us this story.
I could have thrived on livelier repartee,
but it was Ann's nasal and strident conscience
that watered our drinks.
We had to hear how the child never uttered a sound,
and we had to hear how its destitute eyes
lacked even the means of reproach.

Finally, we had to share the ugly triumph
of Ann's blatant self-pity
as she firmly extracted the heavy latch-key
and tossed through the door.

Light

It had been darkening for a while,
but we sat on at the kitchen table,
unwilling to clear the dishes or to turn on the light.
Neither of us had much to say,
but we held hands across the oilcloth
and from time to time
Ian fingered the ring on my finger.
After two years of living together,
who would have thought that marriage
would make a difference?

In the dim light I looked at the things on the table -
the dishes, the glasses, the cups, the electric fry pan -
and I saw in the disorder of their placement
the achieved order of our lives.
What would happen, I asked myself, if I were to lift
my cup from its saucer?
I shook this thought firmly out of my head
and looked up at Ian.

And there was my father seated across the table.
Some faint moonlight defined his silver hair,
and his watery eyes were fixed on mine.
'Please clarify your position,' I heard him say.
He spoke with his old articulated patience,
and he squeezed my hand.
'For a mature student,' he continued, 'yours
is not the best posture.
It's time for Ian to do the dishes
so that you can get back at once
to what passes for your desk.'

I squeezed his hand in return,
and I answered from my heart.
'Father, I say this with love,
and I say it for the highest good:
please go back now to your place of rest
and leave me alone with my life.'

Then, without saying a word,
I stood up as Ian stood up,
and together we left the kitchen.
We passed the small table stuck in the hallway
where my notebook lay open beside a book on torts,
and we entered the door to our bedroom.
We stopped in the dark and Ian let go of my hand,
and I heard him groping in a drawer.
Then he struck a match and lighted a stub of candle
which he placed on the floor by the futon.

I took in my breath as its light
took over the room.

The Lily-White Boys

'Oh God,' said Daphne,
'here come the lily-white boys.'
I got up from the bed to stand behind her
where she peered through the blinds.

The two young men were stumbling over the beach,
burdened by armloads of stuff
but wearing no caps to shade
their Manhattan pallors.

'They'll be burnt to a crisp in that sun,' I said,
sliding my hands in position to cup her breasts
and settling my groin on her bottom.

'I can't believe it,' she said. 'Look what they've got.
They've got wet suits and snorkels
and those flipper things that go on your feet.'

'Not to mention surf boards and beach balls,' I answered.
'And doesn't that square thing look like a picnic hamper?'

It was hard to tell exactly what all they had.
They were only just emerging from the line of palms
that bordered the big hotel.
You couldn't miss them, with their bright blond hair,
but it wasn't easy to see their features;
I had to imagine their looks of fatuous content
as they plodded along with their cargo.

Daphne turned then and kissed me
hard on the mouth.
'Get dressed now,' she said. 'Quick.'

'Hey, what's the hurry?' I answered.
'It's another hour before I have to meet
my kids at the playground.'

'Shit, can't you see that I know those two?'
She broke away and stamped her foot.
'Tom made them promise to look in on me -
in case I got bored.'
At that we both started laughing.
Then we hugged each other and laughed some more.
And then we both laughed so hard
that we had to sit down on the edge of the bed.

'Oh God,' she said, struggling to get her breath
but burying her face in her hands.
'I only hope that that rear window
isn't painted shut.'

Lucky

The men called on Nell that same evening.
They were dark in feature and dark in intent.
She would have been helpless if not for her dog.
It was a mastiff, easily roused,
and easily thirty inches high at the shoulder.

I only missed them, Nell says, by some twenty minutes.
It was a night with no moon and no stars.
I had left Nell's early on my long walk up the valley -
with necessary work at the end
and a promise of seeing Nell the following Thursday.
I was grateful I knew the paths.

One of the men had a short, weaselly build
and a large dark wen on his forehead.
He did all of the talking, his cap in his hand.
His tall companion could have been my twin brother -
I repeat Nell's uneasy description -
a dark twin, a taciturn image of me,
but capable, unlike me, of enormities.

It was a long, lonely hike up through the valley,
removing me one step at a time from Nell.
Oh, she was lucky that she had such a good dog,
luckier than the pensioner down the road
and the young couple from the city in the rented cabin.

Nell's hands no longer shake, she is calmer now.
We say to each other that we are lucky.
Luckier, I suppose, than that dark loathsome figure
moving around out there in the tortuous somewhere,
abroad in the dark hills.

The Match

Her arms were white to the elbows
with a fine dusting of flour.
I carefully kissed her goodbye,
a hand on each shoulder,
and then I picked up my hat.

At the hall door I stopped
to look back in the kitchen,
but she'd turned away.
The faded green in her kerchief
matched the green in her skirt.

On the way out I checked myself at the mirror.
A red spot marked my chin
where I'd cut myself shaving.
The ticket to the match lay heavy
in my coat pocket.

From the kitchen a blast of song
shot through the house.
She wouldn't hear me open or shut the door,
but she'd hear all the top tunes
and news on the hour.

Milk and Cookies

Finally Pam took the job at the library,
and there she fell in love with her handsome Jeff.
Yawning, I shut the book and got off the bed.

Well, that's life, I suppose.
Never a dull moment.

I went to the kitchenette for milk and cookies
and then sat down by the window.
I stretched out my legs and saw again
that my slippers had lost their oomph.

They'd lost their little gold tassels.
They'd lost their bright blue shine.
They'd lost their flavour on
the bedpost overnight.

I'd get a new pair, I thought, but if I do,
the kids will probably send me a pair for Christmas.
That's what I said last Christmas.
That was before they made Joe
a precinct captain.

Joe's card from Tampa lay gathering dust on the sill.
'Having a ball in Florida,' it said,
and It showed a girl in a bathing suit
holding a ball.
Of course they could only go there
out of season.

But that's all beside the point.
I finished my milk and cookies and washed the glass.

I lowered the Venetian blind and got out of my house coat.
Thanks to the coupon sale at Pay 'N Save,
I had my choice of two different kinds,
of bubble bath.

Mona

We found the door of Frank's flat open,
and Mona stood just outside it,
bent toward the door and worrying her bead necklace.
We could hear Frank inside on the phone,
dumping his basket of words in the mouthpiece.
He was telling someone he called Sweetums
that he was able to do it again
now that he had been cured in Lourdes.
Whatever he meant by Lourdes I don't know.
The curing that was done to Frank
I'd say Mona did it,
but there wasn't one word about Mona.

'Come on,' I said to her then, 'let's get out of here.
We've heard enough of this bullshit.'
I took hold of her arm to pull her away,
but Mona just shuddered like an old sick dog.
Then to my disgust she crumpled against the wall
and slumped to the floor.

Meanwhile Frank's voice was farting on
with a load of mush.
Things would be better between them now,
or so he was saying.
He had missed her lips and her eyes
as well as some parts of Sweetums I needn't mention.
You wouldn't want any qualifications to know
those two were well acquainted,
and Mona was starting in to blubber
like a stupid schoolgirl.
She had buried her face in her hands,
and she hadn't bothered to straighten out her dress.

It was twisted up on her legs,
showing off her knees.

'Come on,' I said, 'get your bum up off the floor,'
but she shook her head and kept sobbing.
In fact, with each mouthful of Sweetum's attributes
she sobbed all the louder.
'Come *on*,' I said for the last time,
fed up and ready to leave.
'Will you get on your feet before Frank hears you?
You're making a right show of yourself.'

A Mug of Black Coffee

My first assumption was that my mother
was in her bedroom talking on the phone.
That was how she spent a lot of her time.
She had taken to calling her sister Yvonne in Newark,
the sister she had not set her eyes on
since they both left Utah.
She was also calling her lawyer a lot,
and sometimes her broker,
and of course she called me.

She had called me that morning,
and that was why I was not on hand at the airport
with the rest of the team.
That may be why my firm lost a contract,
but to say so now
would strike you as callous.

My mother also phoned her doctor that morning,
or so she had told me,
and that is why, at seven minutes to ten,
I stood like a fool in her kitchen
yelling to her to hurry it up.

When three minutes had passed, I called out again,
much louder this time.
'Paula,' I called, 'are you coming with me
or are you spending the day on the phone?'

There was still no answer,
and I sat down hard at the kitchen table.
A mug, half full of black coffee, felt warm,
so I spooned in some sugar and drank it down at a gulp.
When another three minutes had passed,
I called out her name again, 'Paula! Paula!'
Then I rose from the table.

I do not know what made me run
up the two flights of steps,
but as the clocks at the airport were showing the hour
(that is how it occurred to me just then),
I was opening the door to my attic playroom.
My mother had left it about as I had left it,
with my toys stored in the gaily painted trunk
and my rocking horse jack standing in the shaft of sun
which pointed down from the skylight.
My swing lay on top of the trunk, but the two hooks
which had held it in place were still screwed in
tight to the tie beam.
The room was about as I had last seen it,
some years before,
except that a rope passed over one of the hooks,
and the lock on the low window
was pulling one end of the rope down toward that window,
and my mother's neck, centered below the hook,
was pulling the other end
down toward the floor.

The Next Day

The next day brought no sign of Emily,
and I sat for long minutes
in the empty summerhouse.

I stared at the phone on the wall,
but I hadn't the courage, or the will,
to lift the receiver.

My old blind beagle lay wheezing on the rug;
he wanted me to whistle him
out for a walk.

I thought of the work to be done on the window:
the cracked pane of glass
I had yet to replace.

I looked again through yesterday's weekly:
horse shows, obituaries, and baseball scores.

If I had a dollar for each time
that I hated Emily,
I would bribe God to give me a better life.

If I had it all to do over again,
I would shoot myself.

Once Again

It was about nine when she reached home,
and I knew at once that once again
she had broken her least favourite
of the Ten Commandments.
It was not so much the late hour -
she did sometimes work late -
as her just definable air
of feigned good will.
In short, she was too polite.

I had eaten already,
and while I turned up the oven on her dinner,
she busied herself brushing snow from her boots
and hanging her coat in the closet.
When I found her viewing the roots of her hair
in the hall mirror,
she was careful to compliment the dry bouquet
I'd arranged on the table.

Then she sat down to her meal,
and I watched her, more or less,
as she dealt with her food.
She looked tired, and I noticed once again
the small lines of worry
spreading out from her eyes.
But she did finish all of the goulash,
and she drank two glasses of wine.

And then, once again,
as I cleared her dishes from the table,
she told me about the problems
she was having with clients.
She repeated them word for word.

When I brought in her coffee,
I could stand it no longer.
I knelt down by her chair
and caught her waist in my arms.
As my heart knocked wildly on my ribs,
I buried my face in her lap.

On the Hour

I was just putting in my new earrings
when the knock came at the door,
but it was Maura, not Donal, who stood there
and I stuttered over my greeting.
Then, covering my confusion, I took her coat
and hung it to dry.
She protested that the coat wasn't wet.
There was no rain really, she said,
just a fine mist.

I pulled a chair over to the fire for her,
and I busied myself with the kettle.
Rain was promised anyway, I told her,
but then we'd had a fair good summer.
There was that in it, she agreed.

I don't recall what else we said
while I got the tea ready,
but I did feel her eyes on my back.
And I don't remember what she was wearing
except that she had on the watch
that Donal gave her for her birthday.
She made a point of looking at it when she said,
'I came right on the hour, you see.'
And she gave me a level look
that I couldn't return.

Then she rose to her feet and walked over to her coat.
'I didn't come for your tea,' she said,
reaching into one of the pockets.
'I came to give you your letter back.
Donal has enough on his plate these days

without having to read something like this
from the likes of you.'

She placed the letter on the kitchen press,
and I stood there caught out,
holding the sugar in one hand
and the milk in the other.

Pale

He looked so painfully pale
as his mother sat there watching him
that I wanted to scream.

I wanted to do more than scream.
I wanted to throw the post card
out the gable window.
It could share its tidings with the old hydrangea.

But the card was held tight in her fat hand,
and she stared and stared at her pale,
beautiful son.

This should have been the moment
for the telephone to ring,
or for Agnes to call in
for morning coffee -
but the cold room focused on our three heartbeats.

Then I dug my fists in my pockets, suddenly scared.
He stood by the sideboard, pale in his beige jersey.
She lifted her hand to her mouth
and spat on the card.

Pints

'Do you really want to marry her?' Michael asked.
The question lay sticky on the table between them.
Desmond reached for his pint, and I
looked down at my feet.
My shoes, as usual, needed a polish.

When I looked back up, Desmond had not replied.
They had nearly finished their pints,
and the look they were giving each other
was an empty stare.
I drank up my pint and went to order my round.

It takes five minutes to fill a good pint.
That's what the barman always tells me.
By the time I returned with our drinks, they had both gone.
They hadn't gone to the gents, they had left the premises.

I sat down with the three pints,
and then I walked back to my room.

I hear that Michael was invited to the wedding,
and I hear that the party went on for three days.
Molly is four months gone now - or so they tell me -
and everyone, as usual, seems to be very happy.

My shoes still need a polish,
and it still takes a full five minutes
to fill a good pint.

A Plain Face

Kit's face was without expression.
'If that is so, Billy,' she said at last,
'what was my part in all this?'
She looked me square in the eye,
as was her custom.

'Your part, your part,' I countered,
'you had no part.'
I was looking, myself,
in every direction.

But I had to say that to Kit,
though I stood there woozy
from my own words.
A server was coming near us with a tray,
and I motioned for wine.

In the silence that came with the wine,
the voices of strangers took over.
Mostly they prated away
about Kit's paintings,
but a man to my left held forth
on the nocturnal habits of lemurs.

Kit still hadn't made reply,
and I drank up my wine so fast
that I had to wipe some excess
from the edge of my mouth.
'Kit,' I began, 'I'd better explain myself.'

'You've made yourself clear, I suppose,'
Kit answered,
at the same time wiggling some fingers
at a new arrival.
Her obvious lack of expression
made her almost pretty.
Plain as it was, her face
was still her best feature.

'I'm sorry,' I said, touching her thin arm,
aware I couldn't keep her attention longer.
'I should have known this isn't
what you need tonight.'

She looked me again in the eye.
'No, but I think you need this.'
She gave me her glass of wine,
then turned to speak to the man
who knows about lemurs.

Pockets

I turned my pockets inside out.
There was little enough to show
from the other side
of the underneath.

Holy, holy, holy,
the Lord God is holy.
So indeed were my pockets.
So were my soles.

What I must do, I decided,
is remake my soul.
I shall take it to the still waters,
where early in the morning, aha,
my song shall rise.

Slowly I slid to a standing position
with more than a little support
from the brick wall.
The world was rearranging its colours
and offering up its usual bits and pieces.
The challenge this day would be to live
by bread alone.

Rachel

Rachel sighed again, but checked herself in mid-breath.
'I'll make us some tea,' I said.

I squeezed her hand and when she didn't respond,
I freed my limbs from the sheets and got up
to walk to the door.
'Some tea would be nice,' she said,
and she gave me a wan little smile.
The smile she gives to the children
when they try to please her.

In the kitchen, I busied myself
while the water boiled.
I cleaned out the sink and hung up the towels.
I wiped off the counters and swept the floor.
The sun shone bright on the plants
in the window boxes.

When I returned, with tea and ginger cakes,
Rachel stood looking out the window.
She had opened the curtains wide.
Like me, she was still naked, and the same sunshine
that had brightened the plants made a halo
around her body.

'Here is the tea, honey,' I said to her,
but she didn't respond.
She was churning the mill in her mind,
grinding the grain of her disappointments
into a finer and finer flour.

'Here is the tea, honey,' I said again.
'Thank you, Stephen,' she answered.

Ralph's Mother

Ralph's mother lived in her bedroom,
two stories removed
from the rough-and-tumble care
of kitchen and garden.

His sister carried up meals
on a polished tray
and brought down small commands
in a cramped, spidery script:
Carry on. Persevere. Prosper.
Mind yourself. Charge.

Ralph bartered these on the street
for tolerance or favour
in our rough, running games.
We traded them with each other
for marbles or gum
till they wore to rags in our pockets.

One day Ned kicked the ball
into Ralph's yard,
and we made him burrow through the shrubbery.
The face he saw in the window
was that of a radiant angel
whose long fingers
reached two stories down
to comfort his sweat-streaked brow.

The Servant

He watched her shake the rain
from her coat and scarf,
the fine drops spattering
the floor of the entry.
She handed the coat to me,
and together they walked in
to the drawing room fire.

I could have told him it would end like this.
No fear of her not coming back.
Not with summer just around the corner
and the old man mad as ever about her.

Not my problem of course.
I hung up her coat and went back to my kitchen.

I could see them plain in my head
as I scrubbed the pots.
He'd have his forefingers hooked behind his back,
and she'd be poking at all those books on the shelves.
She'd only laugh at him if he asked
how she'd gotten on.

I sat down and wiped my face on a cloth.
I was hot from leaning over
the basin of water.
The rain beat hard on the shut window,
and the pain was there in my side.
When the old man came down,
they'd want their tea.

Signing for a Package

I held the curtains apart as the young man
staggered in and set down his burden.
'Someone will have to sign for this,' he said.
He looked like he hadn't shaved that morning,
and his shirt was so tight it pulled on the buttons.
'Just a minute,' I said, and left him.

I was going to ask David to sign,
but he was no longer in his study.
It was a bright morning, coming after the heavy rain,
and a warm breeze was blowing in from the west.
No doubt David, ignoring the doctor's orders,
was out again walking the dogs.

I found the young man seated at the kitchen table
with legs stretched out like the lord of the manor.
'Where would you like me to sign?' I asked him.
He hooked his thumbs in his belt loops and smiled.
'That was a heavy package,' he answered.
'Aren't you going to offer me a drink?'

His eyes were a pale blue and they looked misplaced
under his fierce black eyebrows.
His breath was strong and he smelled of traffic.
But after all these weeks I remember most clearly:
his hands were surprisingly soft,
he had one gold tooth.

By the time that I heard the dogs,
he was, fortunately, gone.
I could never have explained it to David.

Small Favours

It was to be a frustrating afternoon.
That's what Dr. Meriweather said,
easing into an armchair,
folding his hands on his paunch.
When Lydia said that she was inclined to agree,
well I had to laugh.

No, I didn't actually laugh,
but I turned my face to the food.

There was smoked salmon and brown bread
and chicken salad and potato salad
and apples and oranges and nuts
and chocolates and mints.
There was cheddar and brie and a plethora of crackers.
There was sherry and whiskey and gin.

'At least we won't go hungry,' I said,
but I looked around and no one was smiling.
Father was in a dither
and Mother looked put upon by fate.
Old Mr. Todd, the only one to show up
(except, of course, for the good doctor),
sat twisting a paper napkin.

'Oh come on now, everyone,' I said,
'it's not as if anyone died,
and by all accounts we're still legally sane.
Would anyone care for a drink?'

Only Lydia nodded, so I prepared
a gin and tonic stiff even for her,
then poured myself an even stiffer whiskey.
Father stood glaring by the big window,
but Mother, with a drawn-out sigh,
kept stroking the shiny cover
of the doctor's new book.
'Well, here's to you, Dr. M,' I said,
holding the glass of whiskey up to my eye,
'and whatever success the good Lord may grant you.'
Dr. Meriweather, starting to speak, broke into a cough.
Then he patted his coat pocket where, no doubt,
he carried an outline for some impromptu remarks.

'And here's to whatever small favours
the good Lord may send our way.'
I held my glass high in a smart salute,
and Lydia, without a first or second thought,
held hers out too.

A Sour Taste

I eased my hand from under the woman's buttocks -
it had gone numb there -
and began slowly to disengage my body.

'What's the matter?' she said, waking up
and grabbing my shoulder.
'Don't leave me, Arnie.'

Arnie? So that was the name I was using.

Her name was Sheila, I knew that much,
though I couldn't to save my life -
even if I wanted to save my life -
tell you how I knew.

The rain was beating hard on the window,
and the wind howled like a party of caged idiots.
Somewhere out there in the dark
was my smashed-up Porsche.

With a sour taste in my mouth
I rolled over on by back.
The plaster in the ceiling was cracked.
There was no shade on the lightbulb.
My head was beginning to ache.

'Don't leave tonight, Arnie,' she pleaded.
'I'll do anything you ask, only don't leave me.'
She was clutching my arms and kissing my chest.

I closed my eyes so as not to see what she looked like.

A Special Occasion

Hilda is looking down on me now
where they've brought me for lunch at Johnson's,
where we used to bring them
on special occasions.
The roast beef is still tasty
if I take it in small enough bites.

Our sons and daughters are here, with their wives and husbands.
That's Lionel and Marjorie and Elmer and Jeannie.
And that's Harriet and William and Eleanor and George.
They all look chipper enough,
though Elmer has aged since they let him go
at the bank in Hannibal.

I've shown them the letter that came
from my great grandson Ben.
He's off in the Persian Gulf.
He's defending our freedom - so William tells me.
I'm a little bit out of touch.

Hilda is up there smiling
her bittersweet smile at this fresh young kid
she met at the St. Louis World's Fair.
We used to say we would see
one hundred together.

But my brother Roscoe is here -
there in that goddammed wheelchair.
I'm glad to see Roscoe again,
even if he won't let on
that he knows who I am.
It's a good few years since he and I hauled gravel.

The others are all back at the house,
my children's children and some of their children
and some of their children's children.
So many I won't know who's missing
unless someone tells me.
They'll make me tired with their cards and boxes,
and they'll make me blind with their popping cameras.

My gift to them will simply be
that I'm still alive,
and I'll say, as I always do,
that there's nothing like it.

The Summer Dress

Karen stared at me from the doorway.
'I thought Ted and Jean might be here,' she said.
'I've been waiting for them at the mall.'
She was wearing a bright summer dress,
and I knew without asking that she'd bought it
for the day in Seattle.
'I don't understand it,' she said.
'Why would they leave without me?'

She looked so pathetic and pretty
that it nearly shattered my heart.
'Come in for a minute,' I said,
'and let an old man serve you a cup of coffee.
It's only instant, but it may
do you some good.'

Karen looked just right in the dress,
or maybe it's just that I'm still
partial to blondes.
Anyway, as she sat in my kitchen,
the bright colours of the dress seemed to reflect
the colours of her face.
Of course they were meant for Ted to admire, not me.

I gave her the coffee and some sweet rolls
left over from breakfast.
She drank the coffee black, but she wouldn't touch
any of the rolls.
'Look at that sunshine,' she said, pointing to the window.
'It's going to be a lovely day in the city.'

'Let me tell you a little story,' I said in reply,
and I patted her hand.
'There was once a very pretty young woman
whose girlfriend was faithless,
and there was a sympathetic old man.
He was always a bit of a fool
when it came to women,
but he had an even bigger
fool for a son.'

Sundays

Peter didn't appear that afternoon.
But who cares?
I didn't appear either.

The barman told me later he missed us both.

I didn't appear because I was tired.
I was tired of meeting each Sunday in the same bar.
Tired of drinking gins at the same table
in the same dark corner.
Of walking afterward along the river
and ending up in the same small hotel room.
With its sagging mattress and its sanguine drapes.

I was tired of appearances,
and I may have been tired of Peter.
But I don't know why Peter
did not appear.

And I don't know why I'm spending each day-long Sunday
soaking up gin at the bar
and then staring into the river.

This House

I am aware that something
informs this house.
Something bright. A possibility.

I realized it first
mending the linen,
and I felt it again, much later,
counting the spoons.
One night, looking out on a storm
through the leaded window,
I scarcely dared turn.
The air behind me was charged
with staggering promise.

Oh I don't say any of this
to the likes of you,
for I am aware what you think
as you sip my tea
and brush a delicate crumb
from your nervous finger.
And I no longer care that your visits
are seasonally timed.
That you smile too much.
For I am aware of how all
alone you must be.

Now stop quick at my door
and kiss my cheek.
Then turn the ignition key
of the motorcar
that will take you far, far
away from this house.

But take care you don't drop
the apricot jam.
It will do to sweeten the sticky
mouths of your children.

Through the Willows

They're all waiting for Sam
to say something,
but she just sits there picking
at the scar on her arm.
And she looks at the weak light
still glancing the sunflowers
as if there were nothing else
in the whole valley.

It's my opinion, of course, that they think Sam knows
a lot more than she knows,
and I can see Harriet just itching
to rough her up.
Harriet would like that all right,
especially with the twins to help her out.

I could laugh out loud, but then they'd all
be looking at me.

I can imagine Sally laughing at them too -
if I ever get the chance
to tell her about it.

And wherever she is now, I hope she remembers
who bought her the ticket
and whose dress she was wearing the afternoon
she slipped out the French doors
and through the willows.

Uncle

Indefatigable, the cousins
sit listening to yet another
of Mildred's trenchant narrations.
Coffee turns cold in her cup,
and a scone, from which she has yet to take a bite,
flourishes grand to enhance
her purple points.
Uncle always said
that she had a way with language.

At the far end of the room the ancestral portraits
hang stoically from corner to corner.
They are all decently covered, but I imagine
her voice offends them.
I'll bet they're just dying
to turn over in their graves,
but of course I don't say a word.
Uncle always said
that no one would take us for sisters.

Well what can you expect, I say to myself,
buttering another drastic piece of bread
and tuning my ears for a car on the gravelled drive.
Sooner or later this too will pass away.
Mr. Cheswick will come with kind words and papers,
and she'll shut her gob for a time
when he opens his briefcase.
Uncle always said
that silence was golden.

The Visitants

What could I say to them?
That I had been all alone in Vienna?
That I had failed to achieve my purpose?

The subconscious has no sense of humour.
I could have said that, but would it
have been news to them?

And what had they to tell me?
That imagination halts behind reality?
That, I already knew.

In fine, there was little enough exchanged
with those proud figures who walked into my life.
Who appeared at dusk on the garden paths.
Who took shape on late summer evenings
down by the boathouse.

Was it all then a gratuitous visitation?
I have no words of theirs to ponder
as my library draws these autumn afternoons
to its dark mahogany depths.
I have only the conviction of some elusive meaning
in the high carriage of those proud walkers.

Warnings

I was not, I gradually came to realize,
the only one on the road.
I'd been lost awhile in my usual destructive yearning
for Henrietta Jordan.
Henrietta is an ugly name,
but Henrietta Jordan is lovely -
with long auburn hair
and long salacious legs.
Everyone remembers her laugh.

The oncoming car remained for some time
two points of intense light
wavering on the dark, untouchable horizon.
The last time that I saw Henrietta Jordan,
we met by chance in a shop.
Then we walked through a public park
where we drank lukewarm beer
out of plastic cups.
When she came with me back to my room,
it was her own suggestion -
'for old time's sake,' as she put it.
But it wasn't at all like old times.
My fault. Of course. As usual.

It isn't that life doesn't always provide us
with ample warnings.
My friends both told me I ought not to get involved
with Henrietta Jordan,
and I was fully aware, for perhaps a minute,
of the oncoming car.

The Way Ahead

She turned and walked away briskly
in the direction of town.
With my bad leg it was more
than I could do to keep up.
'It wasn't my fault,' I burbled,
acid rising in my throat,
but she didn't moderate her pace,
and she didn't look back.

A passer-by might have felt sympathy,
might have stopped to allay my tears,
but there wasn't a passer-by.
There were only the two of us,
and I couldn't keep up.
There was a long bleak way ahead of me,
and I couldn't keep up.

So I had to kowtow again.
I had, in fact, to apologise at length.
She made me repeat and repeat
how sorry I was.
I had to say it wouldn't happen again
(though it wasn't really my fault).
God help me, I had to get down on both knees
on the wet, stony road
while she sat on a wall and heckled.

The road is as wearisome as ever
and darker now that the stars are clouded over.
But she's walking less fast,
and she's letting me lean on her arm
to maintain my balance.

Though it's starting to rain again,
and a raw wind has risen off the lake,
she says my muffler and gloves
have helped a lot.

When we get back to the flat,
I'll make her a nice cup of Bovril
and draw her bath.

The Weather Report

The voice on the radio spoke
of a Met Office warning:
heavy flooding in areas of Munster
and South Leinster.
Gale force winds would continue.

She turned to me with a smile of sorts.
'I suppose that does it for the golf,' she said.
I looked at my clubs still standing
against the wall by the door.
Did she think she was being sympathetic?

'I don't believe anyone, even your friend Brian,
would play in this weather -
though golfers are, by definition, all crazy.'
She touched her hand to my shoulder as she said this.
Was she trying to be funny?

I crossed the room and looked out on the world.
Small patches of blue were clouding over,
and rain once again was spattering the window.
Her dahlias were beaten flat in their muddy beds.
The apple trees stood in water.

'Why don't we go sit in the living room?' she said.
'I'll build up the fire and make some tea.
We could pull up the sheepskin rug
and listen to the records we bought in Dublin.'
You'd have to give her high marks for effort.

She was, as a matter of fact, doing her best,
and I noticed that she was wearing
the hand-stitched blouse I bought her in Tenerife.
'Give us a big kiss,' she said; 'it won't hurt you.'
So I gave her my very best imitation.

What to Say

I kept up with him and squeezed his arm,
but still I said nothing.
Where would I find the words
to say what was needed?

We plunged through crowds on the footpaths,
stopping briefly where little red men
told us to stop
and then striding out.
Anxious shoppers on their lunch hour
parted for us as best they could,
but a young woman in a dark blue coat
was slammed into a brick wall
and her purchases scattered
through passing feet.

Once he managed to shake me off,
but I caught up at the next corner
and again took his arm.

That was a long time ago.
Today I would know what to say.
That day, I didn't.
My breath was coming in bursts
and my heart was a flapping fish.
I let go when we came to a market
and watched his back as he disappeared
between stalls of apples.